THE RAFT THAT SOARED

Dedicated to kids and families
on the move, everywhere

Dr Rebecca Bower and Steven Ayling

Illustrated by Ajay Lard and Gulce Gokceoglu

Acknowledgements

This story is based on the inspiring work of David Pollock and Ruth Van Reken in their groundbreaking book, *Third Culture Kids* (2001), where they outlined a powerful and important globe-changing RAFT model for supporting families and children in transition. We'd like to thank Ruth for being such a great guide and support for us as we worked through this project. We thank her too for helping us to land such a wonderful publisher and team of people to work with, in particular Pauline, who guided, laughed and brought great honesty to everything we did!

Thank you to our families and friends for supporting us in this process and commenting on some of our earlier versions of the story. We'd like to thank students within the International School of Basel community for reading our manuscript and providing invaluable feedback and soundbites. Thank you to Saniya, Alice, Molly, Ada, Nora, Sophia, Gyani, Alexa and Elena. On that note, we'd like to thank our colleagues, parents and students from over the years, who have helped to build our experiences and who have inspired us to get started on this project.

Last of all, we'd like to thank our wonderful illustrators, Ajay and Gulce, who 'got' our project from the very beginning and brought our pages to life with their skill, passion and craft. We could not have done this without them.

We hope you enjoy reading *The RAFT That Soared* as much as we enjoyed writing it!

Becca Bower and Steve Ayling

We're leaving!

David sensed the words even though no words were spoken. He could see it in his dad's eyes first.

He looked towards his mum for some reassurance, but her eyes confirmed David's horror. A tsunami of emotion swept over him, plunging him into a deep, swirling ocean of hopelessness, far from the safety of everything once familiar.

Unbelievable! Typical! Great! Sahana thought.

Leaving... AGAIN! The sixth time, or seventh? She was losing count. She wished she'd not dared to hope that this time might be different.

She thought they'd at least stay in London for a few years – that this time she could be more at ease, more relaxed, like being four-nil up in a soccer match with only five minutes left to play. Heat rose in her body as tears filled the edges of her eyes. Another broken promise.

Where to this time?

David was a Stayer. He'd always been a Stayer, for as long as he could remember.

He'd had best friends come and go, like waves lapping against a shore. He'd tried to imagine their fears, their anger and even excitement, but inside he'd always felt partly jealous that it wasn't him that was leaving, that he wasn't the one starting an enthralling new adventure. Now that it was his turn, he knew that leaving wasn't easy either. He felt all those feelings at once. It was an emotion no words could describe.

Transition was what David's counsellor, Ms Tianna, called it; moving on, leaving. David had a simpler word for it: loss.

Tears ran silently down his face as David shared his news, sadness and worries with Ms Tianna. She sat with him, listening to what was on his mind. There was a reason he'd chosen her as one of his trusted adults: his fears felt safe with her.

With Ms Tianna by his side, David knew he could get through anything. Even this.

Sahana was a Leaver. She'd been a Leaver for as long as she could remember.

The day had passed with her mind full of the reasons why this move was unfair. Sahana felt numb, yet filled with anger. She couldn't think about anything else and finally broke her silence at the dinner table with the only question she needed an answer to right then: "Why are we leaving – again?"

After an awkward pause, her dad spoke first. "Your mother has landed a job somewhere new. A smaller city, not too far away. It's a place we can call home, a place we can stay. We promise this time."

"Yeah, right!" Sahana sneered. "That's what you said to me the other seven…ty-two times we've moved to our new 'forever' home." Sahana sighed. "I just don't get why you have to spoil everything."

As she stomped off up the stairs, her father called after her. "And Sahana, please keep this to yourself. It's a bit complicated at work right now, so best if no one knows we're leaving."

After school, David took the same route home that he'd always taken, but this time he chose to sit alone on the bus. He usually loved the way the air conditioning in the bus gave him relief from the heat of the Manila sun, but today he wanted the warmth to cocoon him.

As the bus slowed down and came to a halt in the same traffic jam it always did, the lady on the corner of the street waved to the children on the bus. Today, though, David didn't feel like waving back. Instead, he rummaged inside his backpack.

David pulled out his pencil case and took out his compass. He wanted to leave his mark. On the corner of the seat in front of him, he started to scratch the letters of his name. Tears fell from his eyes again as he realised he was damaging part of the place he loved the most: his home.

The following day after school, Sahana went to her swimming training like she always did.

To warm up, she swam twelve laps back and forth in the pool. As she pushed off from the side of the pool, she thought about how her family never 'swam' back. Sahana's technique was not at its best, but her strokes were powerful, fuelled by the energy of her anger.

Mr D was her swimming coach and PE teacher at school. Sahana had not known him long, but he'd become the closest thing to a trusted adult she'd had at her newest school. Today he wanted everyone to practise diving.

As Sahana approached the diving board, she couldn't help but think that her mum and dad were throwing her in the deep end – again!

A week passed.

The sun shone.

The news wasn't such
a shock anymore.

A week passed.

The rain fell.

The secret was too
much to carry.

As the move started to sink in, David found that drawing helped.

He'd always imagined himself like a tree, strong and sturdy, supporting those around him.

How is a tree meant to move? he pondered as he sat out in the garden listening to the birds overhead. *I have my roots her*e.

Carrying the secret around wasn't easy for Sahana.

She found it hard to concentrate in her classes. It weighed her down like an anchor, too heavy for her slender body to stay afloat. She couldn't think about anything else.

She felt hopeless, **ANGRY, disappointed,**

CONFUSED

"Hey, Ms Tianna," David said as he entered her room at break time. It always smelt of coffee and oranges. David couldn't wait to show Ms Tianna his drawings.

"So, how are you feeling?" Ms Tianna enquired.

"I'm nervous. I'm excited. I'm nervouscited!"

Ms Tianna smiled. "Only you could describe two big feelings with one perfect word."

"I also feel a little sad," he added, his head lowering slightly.

"They're all really understandable and normal emotions to be experiencing just now, David. This is big news for you. For anyone." Ms Tianna thought for a moment. "You know, when you get swept up in a whirlpool of emotions and feel like you're drowning, you just need something to hang on to, something to keep you afloat as you navigate across the waters."

Ms Tianna always managed to explain things in a way that made perfect sense to David.

"Hey Sahana," said Mr D when he found Sahana scuffing the ground with her shoes. "I'm sad to hear you're leaving. I thought you might want to talk?"

Sahana could think of nothing worse. "Nah," she responded. "I'm fine." Maybe if she didn't think about it, if she didn't talk about it, it wouldn't happen.

"Sahana, you know, it's okay to feel upset and angry about leaving," Mr D replied with calm reassurance.

"Yeah, but in the end, I still have to get on the plane, fly to some place I've never been before and just be okay with it all – AGAIN! Why am I always the one that has to leave? It's so unfair." She sighed as she kicked more than just the leaves. "I like London. I want to stay here with my friends. Every time life gets good, Mum has to get a new job and ruin everything. I'm sick of it."

Mr D placed a hand on Sahana's shoulder. "I know, kid, I know. What can I do to help?"

"Get my mum to change her mind?" Sahana muttered as she walked back into the school building. She took the longer route to her next class, wishing she could avoid thinking about her dreaded move.

That afternoon, David took out the notebook he'd received as a birthday gift from his gran a month before. He liked it because it had a mysterious wooden craft flying off into a cloud on the front. It somehow helped him to think more positively about the unknown ahead, about the journey not yet taken.

It was where he kept all his notes about the move ahead, and he decided it needed a snazzy name. *My moving journal,* he thought. *No, no catchiness to that at all… Goodbye Philippines, hello new adventures 1? No, too long and still not very catchy.*

He decided he'd come back to the name as he looked through the photos his dad had printed for him.

These were some of his favourite memories: the one with him and George scuba diving in Palawan and the one with the Chocolate Hills in the background. He stuck them in his notebook. Reminiscing about the good times in Manila was bittersweet.

Small tear droplets filled his eyes, not quite enough to drop down his cheeks, but they obscured his view of the happy memories before him as he thought about leaving his friends and favourite places behind.

The remnants of those tears soaked into his pillow as he drifted off to sleep.

That afternoon after Sahana had slumped home, her mum asked her how her day had been. Sahana didn't have much to say, so she just lied instead: "It was fine."

It wasn't fine. Nothing had been fine since the day she found out. Sahana was at least becoming better and better at lying, or so she thought.

She crashed on her bed and reached for her journal. It was her safe space, the thing she could say anything to – like the neighbour's cuddly ginger cat – without judgement or fear of offending anyone.

Dear Diary,

Today SUCKED. I just wish that everything was staying the same. I don't want anything to change. I like my school. I like my friends. I like my house. I don't like my parents. I mean, I do like them, I just HATE that they are making me move again. Why are they doing this to me? It's so unbelievably unfair.

Tears streamed from Sahana's eyes, landing on the scruffy pages of her journal as she finished her last line. She curled up in a ball and fell asleep next to her journal, exhausted.

That night, David had a very strange dream.

The warm, muddy ground squelched between his toes as he walked through a forest of bamboo that towered over him in every colour. The bamboo was growing scarily fast. Before long, David could barely see the leaves at the top; everything around him was swallowed up in a canopy of darkness. He needed to find his way out, and quickly. He started to run as fast as he could towards an opening in the bamboo.

"Nooooo!" David yelled as he realised what was happening. He had sprinted straight into a lake of foaming algae, or at least that's what it smelt like. He heaved and gasped for breath, trying to swim through the sludgy waters. David panicked as he drifted further into the expanding lake.

An unexpected sight calmed his flailing. "Sometimes you just need something to hang on to, something to keep you afloat."

David's eyes widened. The beaver sounded just like Ms Tianna. Before he had time to answer, the beaver had grunted its way to shore and was gnawing through a giant piece of bamboo.

"Your family is waiting across the waters, David. You'll be home soon."

Was the beaver really talking to him? He thought he must be dreaming.

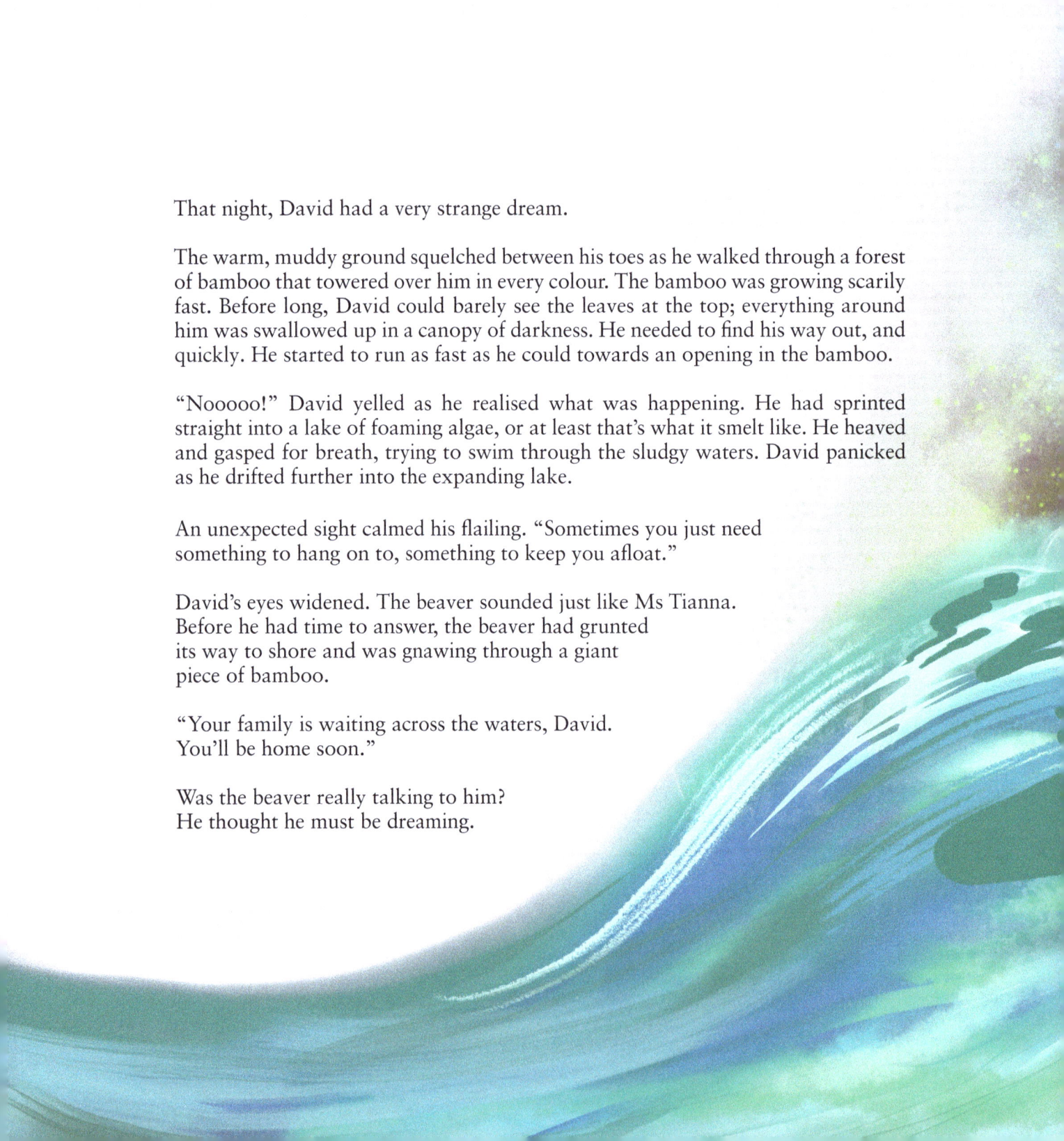

Splaaasssssshhhh!

Bamboo crashed, creating a wave that momentarily submerged David. He coughed and sputtered as he returned to the surface, instinctively grasping the bamboo tightly, not knowing what else he should do. The beaver grunted as he dragged the bamboo – and David – to shore.

"Thank you, thank you," David panted, hoping the beaver might understand. "I just want to go home."

"You can't, you don't live there anymore," said the beaver. "Your family is waiting on the mountainside."

David looked defeated.

"Don't you want an adventure, to go somewhere new?"

"Even if I wanted to, I can't. How am I going to cross the lake?" replied David, thoughts tornado-ing around his head.

"You just have to find a way to navigate the waters. I'll help you, David."

Easy to say when you're a beaver, David thought to himself, but as he wiped the algae from his hair, he had an idea.

That night, Sahana had a very strange dream.

She stood at the edge of a diving board, ready to do something she'd done many times before. Sahana felt confident as she stretched her hands above her head and allowed herself to fall off the edge. Gravity created the momentum, and she closed her eyes in anticipation of entering the water, but the plunge never came.

Freefalling, she opened her eyes to check how far she still had to fall. A wave of disbelief washed over Sahana's body. The water was no longer a crystal-clear pool; she was plummeting towards an ocean of greens and blues.

Splaaasssssshhhh!

Sahana entered the suffocating icy waters. Looking in all directions, she tried to catch her breath before swimming to what appeared to be the shoreline. But no matter how hard she swam, she seemed to be going nowhere. The waves became rougher, salt filling her mouth and stinging her eyes. As she struggled to stay above the water, the safety of the shore drifted further from her reach.

Sahana's arms tired, each stroke an effort in the increasing wildness of the waters. She tried desperately to grab hold of a piece of floating driftwood; she needed something to keep her afloat. But as she dived forward to take hold of it, the waves swallowed her only chance of safety.

The situation was now out of control. Sahana felt desperate. She needed help, and fast. "Help, somebody help!" she yelled, but in the gasping moments between being submerged under the waves, she could see no one else in sight. It was too little, too late.

Darkness crept in as the slimy seaweed below wrapped around her legs. The more Sahana tried to push it away, the more tangled in the squidgy kelp she became. It pulled her further and further down into the ocean, a place so unknown and unfamiliar that Sahana couldn't bear to think what lurked within its murky depths.

She wanted to be anywhere else but here – back to the safety of home. Sahana had no idea how she was going to survive this nightmare.

David woke with a start, sweating.

He finally had something to hold on to. He knew exactly what
he needed to do.

It was Monday, and David was on a mission.

Sahana woke up in a puddle of sweat, her hands clammy and cold.

An uncomfortable mix of anger and sadness took hold of her.
She knew exactly what she wanted to do.

It was Monday, and Sahana was on a mission.

Art lesson finally arrived. The class had been working on perspective drawings and it was time to colour them in, but today David was distracted. Not by his friend Harry for a change, but by a few choice art supplies he couldn't wait to get his hands on. As his classmates set to work on their shading, David approached Mr Coulston about his plan.

"Of course, take what you need, that's no problem," replied David's favourite teacher.

Permission granted, David hurried around the art room gathering all the materials he needed, as well as a few he didn't know he needed: textured paper, glitter, felt squares and stickers. He felt particularly pleased by the decorative edge scissors he'd found amongst the glue sticks.

As the lesson neared its end, Mr Coulston came over to David's desk. "I thought these might be helpful."

David grinned as he took the coloured envelopes from Mr Coulston; he always cared enough to think of the finer details, as all great teachers do.

Lunchtime finally arrived. As Sahana sat eating her cheese and pickle sandwiches, the conversation floated over her head, her mind reflecting on the people around her. Sahana wasn't thinking of fixing anything! She was planning her revenge and knew exactly who was top of her list – her parents.

She turned to her best friend, Jose, and broke her silence.
"I thought you might want to know, I'm leaving."

The news hit Jose like a brick. His face dropped as it dawned on him that his best friend wouldn't be around for much longer.

Meanwhile, for the first time in days, Sahana felt pleased.

Her parents deserved it. Their 'secret' was out.

That week, David spent his evenings busily creating thank you cards, each thoughtfully filled with a message of gratitude. The stack felt heavy in his hands, but in a satisfying way.

He had made thank you cards for Akiko, Harry and Clayton, his besties. He ticked off their names as he went, placing the special peacock card he'd made for Ms Tianna at the back of the pile. It would be the last card he'd hand out.

As David reached for his journal, he noticed the subtle rainbow colours on the back. It reminded him of the many friends and special people he had met and come to love during his unforgettable time in the Philippines.

He tore out a page very carefully from his notebook and set about writing one final and very important letter.

That week, Sahana spent her evenings gathering important items. The stack felt heavy in her arms, but in a satisfying, slightly mischievous way. In the pile was her American School of Barcelona PE shirt (signed in a different life by a bunch of distant people she no longer remembered), her International School of the Hague bear she'd got when back in Grade 1, her current exercise books and a photograph of her standing proudly on her doorstep right here in London.

Sahana and Jose crafted a carefully constructed bonfire in the woods behind Sahana's house.

Before Jose poured lighter fluid over it all, he double-double checked. "Are you sure you want to do this?"

Sahana nodded then struck and dropped the match, creating a flame that neither of them expected to be so big. Sahana was glad Jose had helped her, but she was also okay when he left.

She breathed a little more easily as she emptied the contents of her backpack straight into the fire.

She watched sombrely as her things turned from flames to hot embers and then to cold ash.

The weekend came and David sat with his dad researching their new home. Their fact-finding mission had turned up a few pleasant surprises. He wasn't just going to another country, but a whole other continent!

"David, I didn't know this, but apparently there are stone drinking fountains in every village – with fresh water. You just fill up an empty bottle and off you go!" exclaimed his dad.

David found it hard to imagine. He had never even drunk water from the tap in Manila. "Maybe the water comes from the 7,000 lakes they have?" David thought out loud as he read from the fact-packed webpage he'd found.

"Dad, it also has mountains as high as three hundred skyscrapers!" continued David in his excitement.

"We'd best get some good hiking boots then, David!" said his dad, winking at him.

"Granny told me they make the best chocolate in the world there. Maybe they have real chocolate hills?"

They chuckled.

"What you will get to eat is lots and lots of cheese," Dad continued, his eyes lighting up. "It's hard to get good cheese in Manila."

David's eyes lit up for a different reason. "Oh no, I know what smells occur in this house after you've eaten cheese, Dad!" They laughed and laughed and laughed some more at this!

"They make giant bowls of hot liquid cheese to share," said Dad. "Everyone sits around the bowl, threading bread onto the end of special sticks, like marshmallows. Then they dip it in the cheesy pot, just like the chocolate fountains here. It's called fondue, but by the sounds of it, 'fun-do' is a much better name."

They both giggled again.

David was reminded again why he loved his dad so much, and it was reassuring to feel that they were going on this journey together.

The weekend came.

Sahana reached for her old laptop.

She wanted to find out exactly how bad her new 'home' would be.

Reluctantly, slowly, she typed the destination into the search bar. She paused for a moment, took a deep breath and clicked 'enter'.

Sahana began reading a list of facts. "There are four national languages: French, German, Italian and Romansh." *That can't be right?* she thought. *They don't speak English? This is going to be a disaster.*

She altered her search, this time typing 'beaches'. *There must be something half-good about this place.* She didn't want to believe what she was reading… the country was landlocked. *There's no sea? I'm not even going somewhere with beaches! Not even a beach to make up for leaving my life behind!*

"You have got to be joking," she muttered to herself as she slammed her laptop shut.

That was it. She had seen enough.

The new week came and the days rolled by fast. It was Wednesday afternoon in library class.

As Ms Elarry's softly spoken voice uttered "The End", David remained on the carpet, resisting the invitation of Harry, Soph and Dennis to join them in choosing books. Instead, he pounced on the opportunity to catch a moment with Ms Elarry. "Ms Elarry, you know I'm moving, right?"

As quickly as David had explained what was on his mind, Ms Elarry walked to a shelf of books and ran her finger along the spines. Periodically she tilted a book from the top with her index finger and added it to a rapidly growing pile that rested on her arms. "What a wonderful place to live, David. Wait until you see the treasures that await you." She lifted the pile of books and placed them into David's arms. "Here, take these home and peruse them at your leisure."

Ms Elarry sat down at the computer. David thanked her and began walking away. "One more thing, David. What school are you going to?" As he responded, Ms Elarry tapped away at the computer. "Oh, it looks like a lovely building. We all have fun learning..." she muttered to herself as she scrolled down the page, "and what a wonderful mission statement!"

"Ms Elarry, I think I best go before my arms fall off," David joked. "Thank you so much. I'll bring them back soon, I promise!"

"You best had," said Ms Elarry with a smile. "You're leaving soon and you'll get a fine if you don't!"

The new week came and the days seemed to drag on slowly.

It was Wednesday afternoon in maths class.

As Sahana's teacher was showing the class how to find the value of x using some confusing trig-er-nom-ick equation (or whatever it was called), Sahana's mind wandered for the hundredth time. Thoughts went round and round in her head, like a tumble dryer.

What will my new home be like? It's so unfair. I hope I make some friends. Why me? I can't believe this is happening again. Will I be happy? How long will we stay for? I'm not sure I can do this again. I don't want to do this again.

What if they don't have salt and vinegar Chipsticks? Surely they will have salt and vinegar Chipsticks? **They'd better have salt and vinegar Chipsticks!**

She felt lost. Angry. Sad. Deflated.

Sahana knew she would be leaving soon.

David couldn't believe how quickly another week had gone. He was excited. This was his last weekend before the move, and his family were on a mission to tick everything off their 'list of lasts'.

David and his family took their last walk around the city, ending at Pinkberry Parlour for a giant cup of frozen yoghurt. It was the best one David had ever had and was covered with all his favourite toppings. To end the day, they took in one last sunset, which threw every shade of yellow, pink and orange across the skyline of Manila, far beyond the corrugated rooftops he'd grown to love.

After a busy and emotional weekend, David sat on the sofa surrounded by his favourite photos and the Pinkberry menu he'd taken as a memento that day.

As he busily stuck them into his journal, he knew that he'd treasure the memories of his last weekend for a very long time.

Sahana couldn't believe how quickly her last week had gone. She wished that this was anything but her last weekend in London. Her family were on a mission to tick everything off their 'to-do list' and that list was long and, in her mind, cumbersome.

Sahana and her family set about sorting, tidying, cleaning and packing. There wasn't room for Sahana to take all of her belongings in her suitcase, which meant that her first job was to fill a box with the things she would have to leave behind.

Sadness overwhelmed Sahana as she filled it with toys, books and clothes she knew she would never see again, destined perhaps for a new family or home somewhere that she'd never know.

When cleaning under her bed, amongst the odd tissue and pencil crayon she found a map of the London tube stations. She sat on her bed and traced the routes she'd taken all around London, her hand not letting her drop the map into the box of no return.

After a busy and emotional weekend, Sahana's family sat around the table with her favourite dinner – fish and chips. Sahana tried, but she didn't have the stomach to eat it.

Her last weekend was one she'd rather forget.

David's last week at school was a whirlwind, with time seemingly racing towards his departure.

It was Thursday and the end of the school day. As David got up from his seat to leave the classroom, his mind was filled with what was coming next. He looked around the room, knowing that his next day in this very classroom would also be his last. He put on his jacket, which contained an important envelope with no name.

David let his friends get on the bus before him, then stepped on for the penultimate time. He tried his best to smile as he nervously handed the envelope to the bus driver. "I'm sorry about the seat," he said in a particularly quiet voice.

The bus driver initially looked confused, but he took the envelope and smiled knowingly as David took his seat.

David felt relieved. He was glad his friends were coming home with him today for a final playdate.

Sahana's last week at school was a whirlwind, with time rushing towards her departure.

It was Thursday and the end of the school day. As Sahana got up from her seat to leave, Mr Tanaka asked her to come over to his desk. "Sahana, I want you to know that we are really going to miss you in our class. I know tomorrow will be a big day for you and I've been thinking, is there something special you'd like to do? We could read your favourite story again or play Heads Down, Thumbs Up together in class?"

Sahana looked down at her shoes. "I don't know. Maybe. I'll think about it. Promise."

"No problem," said Mr Tanaka. "You can have as much time as you need to say your goodbyes tomorrow."

"What are you up to?" said David's little sister, Hannah, interrupting things. She had a habit of doing that, especially when David was in the moment, enjoying himself with his friends. "Is it someone's birthday?"

David figured that if he just ignored her for a little while longer, Hannah would leave them alone. He figured right. "Goodbye," David mouthed as his sister turned her back and left.

As Hannah walked out of the kitchen, David saw the faces of his friends and felt bad. He called after her, knowing he shouldn't take his emotions out on his little sister. "Hey, Hannah, I'm sorry for being mean. We're making something to give to our classmates. You can have one later, okay?"

David continued decorating the cookies with his friends. They smelt so chocolatey it made his stomach rumble. But that wasn't the only reason his tummy turned. Tomorrow was his last day and this was his last playdate with his best friends.

"Goodbye, Ginger Cat." That's what she called him. Ginger Cat had no collar, but Sahana knew it was a male cat because, well, she could just tell.

Ginger Cat, or GC for short, cuddled closely to his best friend. The neighbour's cat often liked to visit their garden. So fluffy and warm on her lap.

"Hey, GC, I haven't told anyone yet how I really feel. I'm really worried. I hope I can find a new football team. A new swimming team. I hope we stay longer than a year. I hope this can be my last move for a while. I hope I make new friends. I want to feel at home there." *But I don't feel like I know where or what home is anymore*, she thought.

As she ran her fingers through GC's fur, her eyes filled with tears that ran down her face, slowly at first. GC nuzzled in a little closer, like he was the most understanding entity in the world and knew exactly what Sahana needed right then.

Though it was a special moment that Sahana would always treasure, they would never see one another again.

David felt peaceful, calm and content as he walked into school for his final day, cookies and cards in hand.

As the day wore on, he must have given out at least fifty smiles and embraces, and as his journal filled with emails, phone numbers and messages, his old t-shirt grew less and less white, filled with messages of love, friendships and fond farewells.

He didn't know it then, but that shirt would follow him all around the world, wherever he went.

David took a moment and looked at all his friends around the classroom, breathing it all in.

Goodbye for now, he thought.

Sahana couldn't believe that her last day had arrived. She felt overwhelmed with sadness as she walked into her classroom, hands in her pockets and shoulders hunched up. Knowing that this would be a day of lasts, she would spend the day pretending it was anything but.

At the end of the day, Sahana was asked to stand at the front of the class to be presented with a memory book from all her classmates. She was going to miss her friends, but she couldn't bring herself to look inside, not yet anyway.

Another book for her memory box, her collection of memories from all the places she'd once lived in and loved. This one, she promised herself, she'd never burn.

And she kept that promise.

Goodbye, she simply thought.

David woke after a peaceful sleep.

Today's the day.

Sahana felt like she hadn't slept a wink. It had been one of those nights.

Today's the day.

David set sail through the sky on a raft made of hope,
excitement and nervous flutters.

Sahana took off into the starry night,
her mind full of mixed emotions.

Not long after a smooth landing, David could feel the beat of excitement in his heart, like the soft bumps of luggage landing on the conveyor belt, as he took in the new sights and sounds of his new surroundings.

I hope this move turns out okay.

After a bumpy landing, Sahana's thoughts went around and around, like her suitcase on the conveyor belt in the arrivals lounge.

I hope this move turns out okay.

The six-week summer
holiday had flown by.

The first day of school rolled around,
just like they always do.

David walked in through the large glass
doors of his new school, and there he
met his first new friend.

The six-week summer holiday had been full of ups and downs, twists and turns. But sure enough, the first day of school rolled around, just like they always do.

Sahana walked in through the large glass doors of her new school in Basel, and there she met her first new friend.

"Hi, I'm David," he said, smiling.

"Hi David," she said, smiling back. "I'm Sahana."

RAFT Building

R is for 'Reconciliation'

Reconciliation means 'saying sorry'.
Why is it good to fix and make things right with other people before you leave for somewhere new?

A is for 'Affirmation'

Affirmation is about noticing what and who we are grateful for and letting them know what we appreciate about them.
Why is it good to say thank you and show our gratitude to special people before leaving?

F is for 'Farewell'

Farewell means 'goodbye for now', to the people, places and possessions that have been important to you.
Have a think about why it's important to plan your goodbyes ahead of time.

T is for 'Think Destination'

Think Destination is about thinking ahead to your new school, home and country.
Why do you think it's worthwhile to plan ahead, to think about and research the new place before you leave?

RAFT Spotting Quest

For each of the prompts below you can talk them through with a friend or trusted adult or simply journal them in this section.

Reconciliation

Do you think David and Sahana do a good job of saying sorry and fixing things with those around them? How do the ways David and Sahana make things right (or not) impact their respective transition journeys?

Personal reflection
Who might you want to say sorry to if you were leaving? Is there anything else you'd like to fix? Is there anything you'd want to forgive yourself for prior to leaving?

Affirmation

Where in the story do David and Sahana say thank you and/or show gratitude to the people who are important to them? Which moment of gratitude in the book had the biggest impact?

Personal reflection
How and why might thank yous look different for different people? How would you want to show that you are grateful to those who are important to you when you leave?

Farewell

Who do you think does a better job of planning their farewells in the story, David or Sahana? Why? David and Sahana didn't just say goodbye to people in the story, so why is it important to say goodbye to places and things too?

Personal reflection
If you were leaving, who and what might you want to say goodbye to when leaving and why?

Think Destination

What helped David and Sahana begin and carry out their research? Who do you think felt more prepared for moving somewhere new and why? What are the benefits of researching where you are moving to?

Personal reflection
If you were moving somewhere new, how would you begin your research and which trusted adults would you turn to to help you out? What would you most like to find out about?

The RAFT That Soared

Reflections

Stayers and Leavers

At the beginning of the story, David and Sahana were referred to as a **Stayer** and **Leaver**, respectively. What do you think these terms mean?

Have you ever been a **Stayer** or a **Leaver,** or known someone who has? How did that feel? How might this status change over time?

What are some of the positives and some of the challenges of being a **Stayer** or a **Leaver**?

How might being a **Stayer** impact your feelings about a place after a good friend leaves?

What are some of the hardships that the **Leaver** might face? What strategies might a **Leaver** implement to help themselves cope?

Mixed Emotions

How did David and Sahana feel about leaving? How were their feelings similar and how did they differ?

Do you think David and Sahana's feelings are the kinds of emotions to be expected when moving? What other feelings might someone have about leaving?

How were other characters in the story impacted by David and Sahana's transition?

Coping Strategies

What coping strategies did David and Sahana use to help them manage their big emotions?

What else could they have done that might have helped them better manage their feelings?

David accepted a lot of help from his trusted adults. Who are your trusted adults and what are the characteristics you look for in a trusted adult?

Transition Journey

What are the similarities and differences between David and Sahana's transition journeys?

Do you think either David or Sahana have any regrets? What might they be?

In the middle of the story David and Sahana had some strange dreams. What do you think the dreams might represent?

If you could meet David or Sahana, what top tips would you give them as they prepare to move and settle into a new place?

Thinking about the other characters in the story, what pieces of advice would you like to share with them?

My RAFT Journal

We've shared our story with you. Now it's your chance to tell your story.

Create your RAFT and soar into your new adventure!

There is no right or wrong way to build a RAFT. This is your RAFT, so think creatively, have fun and build it your own way.

Don't worry if it's a bit messy or if everything isn't spelt perfectly – that's not what this journal is about. Make it your own by sticking things on, making collages, printing photos, drawing, and writing down your very own transition plan.

RAFTastic!

So, you're not going to build an actual raft with logs, rope and sweat... but that doesn't mean it's not fun to design what it would look like if you did! Get your best design mind on and draw, scribble and label your raft into reality.

You know, Sahana, I once had a really odd dream about a RAFT...

No way, really?! Me too! What was yours like?!

My transition journey

Everyone has their own unique transition journey, made up of places that have been part of their life story.

Where has your transition story taken you so far? Map out your journey, making it as detailed as you like. You might want to include dates, flags or drawings that remind you of those places.

It doesn't matter if your journey is long or short; what matters is that it's all yours.

I'd have seven destination stops on mine!

It's a good job you have teeny-weeny writing, Sahana!

Express yourselfie!

Transitions can bring up lots of different emotions, just like it did for David and Sahana. Guess what? Here's the good news... there are no wrong or bad feelings to feel. They are all absolutely one hundred per cent okay emotions to experience. So, express yourselfie! To show how you're feeling about your move, draw, take photos (selfies), write, cut out pictures from a magazine, make up lyrics to a song or write a poem.

I remember feeling different emotions when I moved. Nervous and excited... 'nervouscited' to be absolutely precise.

I see a challenge, Sahana! Can you create your own unique word that describes your... 'feelions'?

Dear Diary...

It's good to get your feelings out. This space is for you to express your emotions. Use this page when your feelings are strong and you need an outlet. Doodles, drawings and words are all welcome here...

Who's got your back?

Managing all the feelings that come when moving somewhere new is easiest when you let others know how you feel and when you ask for help. There will be lots of trusted adults inside and outside of school who want to support you. The question is, which trusted adults will you call on to support, guide, help and encourage you with your move? Keep five on hand!

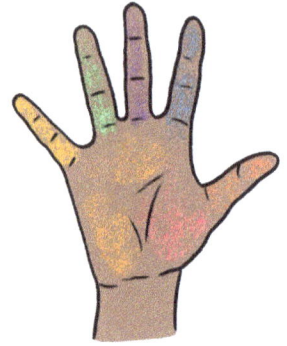

> I think Mr D knew he was one of my trusted adults. I'd put him on my pinky.

> It doesn't hurt to let them know, though. How many fingerprint signatures do you think I could get from my trusted adults?!

Strategy suitcase

It's a pretty smart idea to have a suitcase of coping strategies that you can use whenever big feelings start to overwhelm you. The good thing about this suitcase is that there's no weight limit! You can fill it up as much as you like. Coping strategies are anything that help you feel calmer. It might be taking a deep breath, reading a book or cuddles with a pet.

You know, I actually have a bag of stuff I didn't burn, and that makes me happy. It's my 'feel good bag'!

Way to go, Sahana! Me too. I made mine with Ms Tianna. I have a fidget toy, photos of the Chocolate Hills and some mindful colouring sheets!

Not so daft RAFT draft

Over the next few pages, you will find yourself doing lots of planning. To feel good about your move, it's important to know exactly how and when you're going to carry out your RAFT plan. These pages will help you ensure that there's time to do everything you'd like to do. First things first, though. Follow the three-step process that's on the next page.

Oh yeah, and we know you're busy, but don't forget your mum's birthday too, or to feed your goldfish, or to put the milk back in the fridge… and to brush your teeth – you get the idea!

MONTH:			YEAR:			
SUNDAY	**MONDAY**	**TUESDAY**	**WEDNESDAY**	**THURSDAY**	**FRIDAY**	**SATURDAY**

1. **What's your moving date?** This date should be the last date on your calendar and the first date you put in at the end of the second calendar page. Now you can fill the rest of the dates in – backwards!

2. **Check plans with your family.** Your family will probably have arranged some plans already. Check when they are and make sure they're in your diary.

3. **Revisit this page and add to the calendar** whenever you add something to your RAFT plan.

This looks like a page made for pencil.

Haha! Good idea… easy erase means easy to change!

MONTH:			YEAR:			
SUNDAY	**MONDAY**	**TUESDAY**	**WEDNESDAY**	**THURSDAY**	**FRIDAY**	**SATURDAY**

Reconciliation

Definition

Fixing things and making things right with other people before you leave for somewhere new.
This might mean saying sorry for something. It might also mean forgiving yourself.

Fix it first

Don't worry, we all have to apologise sometimes. No one is perfect. Not one person. Everyone has done and said things they wish they hadn't. The important thing is to make things right with the people you think you may have hurt – before leaving. This isn't the easiest step in the RAFT process, but fixing situations and relationships means you'll leave feeling more peaceful.

Yeah, honestly, that letter saying sorry to the bus driver felt good.

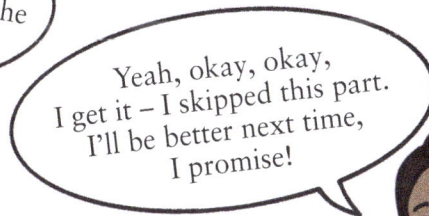

Yeah, okay, okay, I get it – I skipped this part. I'll be better next time, I promise!

Patching it up

Create your own patchwork quilt of apologies. Each square you add can represent a situation you want to fix or a person you want to apologise to. In the square you will also need to think about how and when you'll do this. Don't forget to put it in your calendar! You'll feel so good for making things right.

After apologising, I'm going to stick coloured paper over the top, like a real patchwork quilt.

You'll see all the tricky stuff turn into something beautiful.

Don't sweat the regret

It's best to leave any regrets behind – carrying them around is heavy work. Of course, you can reflect on what you wish you had done and take that learning with you, but save your shoulders from the weight of regrets by forgiving yourself. What are your regrets? Write each one on a slip of paper and stick it in the Bye Bye Basket. Your regrets can stay there as you move on. You can even rip them up first.

This is an activity you won't *regret!*

You're so punny, David.

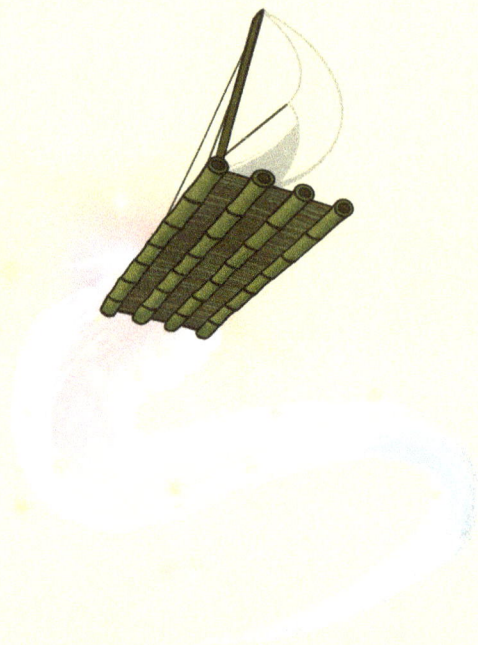

Affirmation

Definition

Expressing thankfulness and gratitude for people, places and experiences. Affirmation is letting other people know that you appreciate them – by showing or telling them how and why you do. It's not just other people, it's important to recognise what you are thankful for in yourself too.

Celebration station

It's time to pause and think how much you have achieved in the time you have been where you are just now. Think of the obstacles that you have overcome, goals you've nailed, successes you've had and moments you are proud of.

How will you display your trophies, medals and certificates of fabulousness? Get creative in representing what you have achieved!

I really got a lot better at swimming. Did I ever tell you that I won a silver medal, David?

Well done! Give me a moment, I'm still thinking!

Gratitude is the best attitude

No doubt your mind is full of all the things you'll miss about your home just now. Those are probably the things, animals, people, places and experiences you're thankful for too. Use this space to express your gratitude through drawings, collage and/or photos. Be specific in writing down the reasons why you're thankful.

Rays of thanks

There are many different ways to say thank you to the people you appreciate and who have been important during your time in the place you're leaving. Add your ideas to the sunshine. The more ways, the more rays. The brighter you'll feel, the brighter the sunshine! When thinking about ways to thank people, think about what they love and what's important to them.

Ways to say thank you

Did you know the word for thank you in Tagalog is *salamat*?

No 'ray', David!

My thank yous!

Don't forget to put this in your calendar

Person I want to say thank you to	What I appreciate about this person	How I want to thank them	Things I will need to prepare	When I plan to say thank you

I got this!

Yes, you have got this! Your upcoming transition is manageable, even though you probably have lots of big, mixed emotions about it. You have lots of trusted adults to support you, but you can also be your own cheerleader. Maybe it feels a bit awkward at first, but it's important to be as kind to ourselves as we are to others. Commit your 'I ams' to paper, using the affirmation station…

I am… ermm. Umm, I am…

Sahana, I can help get you started – there's loads! You are… imaginative, friendly and fun.

Farewell

Definition

Saying goodbye to people, animals, places and things.

List of Lasts

As you say goodbye to places and things, think of what and where you'd like to visit, one last time. It could be anywhere or anything (e.g. a food stall, park or hiking trail). You can use your list to make sure you tick off each of these important lasts and say goodbye properly before you leave. Don't forget to take some photos when you go!

MY LIST OF LASTS	DATE
Last day at school	

Should I put these on my calendar?

Unless you have the memory of an elephant... yes!

Goodbye, for now

As your moving day comes closer, you'll want to say goodbye to all the people who have been important to you. These might be people in school – for example, your friends, peers and teachers. They might also be people outside of school, like neighbours, sports coaches, babysitters or music teachers. Who else can you think of?

Ways to say goodbye

I made about 13 cards!

I didn't make any... but at least I said goodbye to Ginger Cat.

Meeeooooww! (That meant "I'll miss you too, Sahana" in cat language!)

Don't forget to put this in your calendar

Person I want to say goodbye to	How I want to say goodbye	When I plan to say goodbye	Things I will need to prepare

Memory wall

What are some of the many special, important and fun memories that you have made in the place you live just now? Make sure you record some of the highlights, funny stories and happy memories. This is your memory wall, so think outside of the box. You can stick photos, tickets and mementos on, add drawings, comic strips and news stories, or use any other creative way to record those best bits!

Sorry, GC, but when I was stroking you, I may have kept a bit of your fur and, ahem, I may have stuck it in my book too!
Meeoowyuk!
Ooh, gross… hey, I once knew a kid called Alvin who used to stick his boogers in a special bogey book!*
*Spoiler alert for new book incoming, written by Steve Ayling!

For keepsake!

When you're leaving a place that you've lived in for a long or short time, there are often little treasures and mementos that remind you of those special times, places and memories. Whether it's a yearbook, tickets, photos or something from nature, why not put them all together in a special memory box? You can look through your box whenever you like. Use this space for your treasure box mind mapping, planning and/or collage-creating fun.

Goodbye graffiti

There's nothing better than reading a handwritten message from the people who are important in our lives. Use this space to collect memories in the form of messages from the people who care about you. This is a space to collect messages or signatures from those people. A top tip is to stick an envelope front down on the page and keep all the messages inside. Seal with a sticker until you want to read them.

Contact contracts

Goodbye doesn't mean you'll never see or speak to someone again, especially your closest friends. Make sure you have ways to keep in touch after you leave by getting their contact details. Chat to your friends about how you'll stay connected; it could involve old-school snail mail, emails, messages or even gaming together. Draw or stick on a photo of you with your friend. They might even be up for signing your agreement about how you'll keep in touch. A fun way to do this is by drawing a symbol that means something to you both.

Friend

Telephone Number

@ Email Address

Friend

Telephone Number

@ Email Address

Friend

Telephone Number

@ Email Address

Friend

Telephone Number

@ Email Address

Friend

Telephone Number

Email Address

Friend

Telephone Number

Email Address

Friend

Telephone Number

Email Address

Friend

Telephone Number

Email Address

Friend

Telephone Number

Email Address

Friend

Telephone Number

Email Address

Think Destination

Definition

Thinking about the place you are moving to. This is when you do research to find out information about your new country, new school and new home.

It's a matter of fact

You're moving somewhere new! Maybe you know lots about that country, city or village, or maybe you know very little. Either way, now is a great time to find out more. What is it that you'd love to find out?

 I'm moving to:

Capital City:

Flag of:

Weather:

Local Language(s):

 Closest airport:

Local Currency:

 Sahana, this would be a great place for Two Truths and a Lie.

As a matter of 'fact', it would!

Controller

You can't change the fact that you're moving. That's a decision that for now is out of your hands and on your parents' controller. The good news, though, is that there are many things about your move that *are* within your control. For example, maybe you can decide how your new bedroom will look? You may want to sit down with a trusted adult in order to think through what the buttons represent on your controller.

_____ 's controller

Inner detective

The more curious you are about your new home, the better. Learning about where you're going will help make your move much less scary and give you more to look forward to. Even if you've lived there before, you're older now and different things will be important for you to explore. Channel your inner detective and explore all that your new home has to offer. What have you found?

Well, I discovered that Switzerland is landlocked and doesn't have a proper beach... but I've got to say, it's pretty awesome anyway!

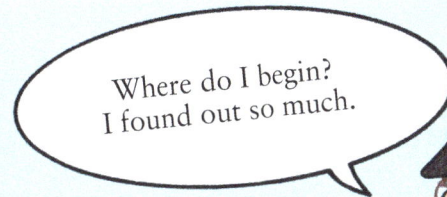

Where do I begin? I found out so much.

Scoping out my new school

Once a decision has been made about which your new school will be, it's time to find out more about it. Use this space to gather all the information you find. You might include the website, print photos, sketch the mascot or write down your favourite part of the mission statement.

What I will wear on my first day of school

List of things I need for my
first day at school

My mum suggested I put my 'smile and positive attitude' on the list of things I need for my first day.

Haa! My mum suggested I include that in my plan of 'what to wear'. Cheesy, but not the worst idea, David!

First impressions count

A new school is an opportunity to make new friends. What first impression do you want to make at your new school? You only have one chance to make a first impression!

My three guiding words for starting at my new school are...

I will be...

Questions I can ask my new classmates

You know, I play a word association game to remember new people's names! Super Smiley Sahana.

That's a great idea, David. I didn't think of myself as smiley before. I'll try and use their name as much as I can when talking with people... David!

Being a friend to myself

You may have thought about 'being kind' as one of the ways that you could make a great first impression? It's important to be kind to others, but it's also important to be kind to yourself. What words of encouragement and support can you say to yourself as you start your new school?

You got this! Smile. You can do this!

Be you! You're great.

Not everything needs to change

Family rituals, routines and traditions are really important. Just because you're moving, it doesn't mean you need to leave these behind. What do you do as a family or celebrate together that you'd like to continue doing in your new home? This is a great chance to talk to your family and make a plan together.

In our new place, I'd like it if we can still…

My new home

This is a page to complete after you have moved to your new home. You can complete your RAFT journey by drawing pictures or sticking on photos of yourself in your new home.

You did it! You made the leap.

Hey, yeah, down here. We're proud of you too. You did it!

Dr Rebecca Bower

Becca grew up in a small village in Lancashire, England. After finishing secondary school, her studies took her gradually north and, eventually, right across the border into the bonnie land of Scotland. "I'll only be here one year," she said. Seven years of friendship and memory-making followed, and Scotland holds a very special place in her heart. It was here that she studied to be a clinical psychologist, specialising in supporting children, young people and their families to thrive.

Becca's RAFT soared to Switzerland in 2018, where she moved to be with her Swiss partner. He has since been working tirelessly to master her perfect cup of home comfort – tea! After all, 'you can take the Lancashire lass out of the UK, but you can't take the UK out of the Lancashire lass'. Becca loves embracing every new and exciting opportunity in Switzerland, be it climbing mountains, soaking in a whey bath, goat trekking or sleeping in the straw. Although she misses her friends and family in the UK a lot, she looks forward to returning home to see them and sharing the beauty and adventure of her new home with them.

England, Scotland, Switzerland... and as Becca says: "There's always space for one more place to call home."

Steven Ayling

Steve had a pretty stable period growing up, born in Birmingham, England, where he lived in the same house for the first 18 years of his life. He set sail for Plymouth to attend university and after seven years began deeply diving into the RAFT process when he moved halfway across the world to the Philippines to work in his first international school setting and complete his Master's degree. Similar to Becca, he declared to his friends and family that he'd be back in a year or two, but fifteen years later he's still there, now married to his wonderful wife Natalya and with two amazing children, Sahana and David (just kidding – they're Soph and Eva!).

However, over all those years, Steve remained connected to his roots, and he continued to have an avid love for English football – watching, coaching and playing. Despite growing up with the notoriously unpredictable and often chilly English climate, Steve can now be seen reaching for a jumper or cardigan in the height of the Swiss summer, thanks to his long stay in the Philippines. He adorns his house with winter decorations at the first sight of a 'ber' month and starts many sentences with "In Manila…." After 15 years of life in Manila, a huge part of Steve's heart still belongs to the Philippines and, as with many cross-cultural students and families, when asked 'where is home?' it's a complex answer packed with emotions.

Both Steve and Becca are proud members of the International School of Basel community, where Sahana and David finally meet. This is their first journey into publishing but they are excited to share future projects in the not too distant future.

Praise for *The RAFT That Soared*

As a Third Culture Kid (TCK), parent of TCKs and TCK educator I can say unequivocally how excited I am to see *The RAFT That Soared* be shared with the world. When my father, David, created the RAFT, his desire was for the crucial, research-informed model to 'sail' far and wide. He never copyrighted this work nor asked for anything in return; his desire was that TCKs and their families everywhere would have access to a healthy transition process. I believe David would be delighted to read this story and to share it with globally mobile families. Thank you for this creative tribute to his legacy!

Michael Pollock

Third Culture Coach and co-author of
Third Culture Kids: Growing Up Among Worlds

The RAFT That Soared provides an opportunity to consider different responses children can have to physical mobility. Even more importantly, by breaking down David Pollock's classic RAFT model into clear, interactive exercises, each reader can personalize how their own story is going. It offers opportunity to both say a 'good goodbye' as well as prepare for a 'good hello' in the new place. This book is a welcome addition to the world of global mobility and needs to be a standard tool for educators and parents alike to use with the children in their care. Well done!

Ruth Van Reken

Co-founder of Families in Global Transition and co-author of
Third Culture Kids: Growing Up Among Worlds

The RAFT That Soared delves into the range of real and sometimes very raw emotions that can impact a child's ability to transition well as they learn about and come to terms with their upcoming move. As someone who has a personal passion for helping parents and specifically children 'thrive', or in this case 'soar', *The RAFT That Soared* is a thought-provoking story and excellent resource for supporting people through the various stages of their transitions, all around the world.

Michael Borba, Ed.D

Author of *Thrivers: The Surprising Reasons Why Some Kids*
Struggle and Others Shine

www.ingramcontent.com/pod-product-compliance
Lightning Source LLC
Chambersburg PA
CBHW061223270326
41927CB00024B/3479

9 781915 264046